GRAPHIC DISCOVERIES
SPECTACULAR SHIPWRECKS

by Gary Jeffrey

illustrated by Claudia Saraceni

The Rosen Publishing Group, Inc., New York

Published in 2008 by The Rosen Publishing Group, Inc.
29 East 21st Street, New York, NY 10010

First edition, 2008

Designed and produced by
David West Books

Editor: Gail Bushnell

Photo credits:
4b&5t, 44all, 45t, NOAA; 6-7all, 45tr, OAR/National Undersea Research Program (NURP); 45b, U.S. Navy photo by Photographer's Mate 1st Class Chadwick Vann

Library of Congress Cataloging-in-Publication Data

Jeffrey, Gary.
   Spectacular shipwrecks / by Gary Jeffrey ; illustrated by Claudia Saraceni.
      p. cm. -- (Graphic discoveries)
   Includes bibliographical references and index.
   ISBN-13: 978-1-4042-1091-2 (lib. bdg.)
   ISBN-13: 978-1-4042-9598-8 (6 pack)
   ISBN-13: 978-1-4042-9597-1 (pbk.)
   1. Shipwrecks--Juvenile literature. I. Saraceni, Claudia. II. Title.
   G525.J445 2007
   910.4'52--dc22

                      2007004760

Manufactured in China

CONTENTS

HOW DO SHIPS GET WRECKED?

Ships are lost at sea for many reasons. Bad weather and striking underwater objects such as reefs or running aground in fog are the most obvious. Other reasons include sinking in battle, piracy, scuttling (sinking a ship on purpose by opening the seacocks), fire, and navigational errors.

AMAZING AND BIZARRE

Other, less likely, causes range from simple carelessness to the very strange. In 1545, the English flagship, *Mary Rose*, capsized and sank as it advanced into battle. The inexperienced crew had left the gunports open. As the ship heeled over to change tack, it filled with water which surged through the gunports as they went below the waterline.

Surprisingly, shipwrecks can sometimes appear on land. In 1883, a gigantic wave created by the eruption of the volcanic island Krakatoa lifted the steamship *Berouw* over a mile (1.6 km) inland and 30 feet (9 m) above sea level!

Ice can be a deadly shipwrecker, as most of it lies unseen underwater. In 1912, the *Titanic* struck an iceberg and sank within three hours. In 1915, the *Endurance*, on an expedition to Antarctica, was crushed by the force of the surrounding ice pack.

The most amazing cause for a shipwreck must go to the Nantucket whaling ship *Essex*. Destroyed in 1820, it sank after it was attacked by an 80-ton sperm whale 2,000 miles (3,200 km) from the west coast of South America.

A late 17th-century engraving shows a shipwreck and a whale. Apparently, fanciful tales of monsters attacking ships were not always make-believe.

Rocky coastlines with strong tides were very dangerous to shipping during the age of sail. People living in these places relied on shipwrecks as a source of income by collecting the goods that got washed ashore. They were known as wreckers (above).

A photograph (right) shows Endurance trapped in the ice pack of the Weddell Sea, Antarctica. The expedition's leader, Shackleton, made a daring journey in a small boat to get help. All the crew members were eventually rescued.

The remains of the most famous shipwreck of all time, the Titanic, (left), were found in 1985.

Diving suits, which had air pumped down to them through pipes from the surface (below), were replaced when the aqualung came along. Improvements to this design created the SCUBA–Self Contained Underwater Breathing Apparatus (above).

This 16th-century painting (above) shows a person being lowered into the sea in a diving bell. Diving machines, like this simple Lethbridge design (below) from 1715, allowed little time underwater as they had no fresh air supply.

DIVING TECHNOLOGY

The Jim diving suit (above) protects the diver from pressure at depths of 2,000 feet (600 m) or more.

Robert Ballard used submersibles, like Alvin (below), to visit the Titanic wreck at a depth of 12,500 feet (3,800 m), in 1985.

Remote-controlled subs with lights and cameras, like MIR (bottom right), explore wrecks without risking human life.

The technology that allows us to breathe underwater has greatly increased our ability to discover the hidden treasures beneath the waves.

EARLY DAYS

Divers began to explore the seabed in the 16th century, after the invention of a watertight diving bell. Soon after, leather diving suits with air pumped down tubes could be used at depths of 60 feet (18 m). By the 1830s, watertight diving suits allowed divers to work safely.

PRESSURE

Diving to greater depths created breathing problems until the aqualung was invented, in 1943. To dive really deep, where the pressure can crush a person, special suits and submersibles are used, which allow scientists to go more than 14,000 feet (4,200 m) deep.

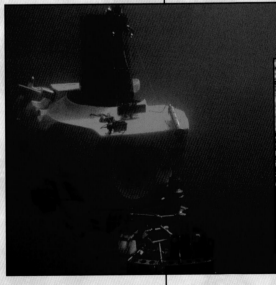

THE RAISING OF THE MARY ROSE

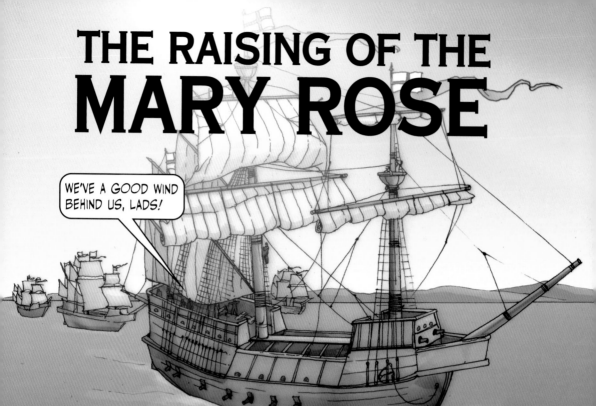

JULY 19, 1545, PORTSMOUTH HARBOR, ENGLAND. FLAGSHIP MARY ROSE LEADS OUT THE ENGLISH FLEET TO FIGHT THE FRENCH FLEET IN THE ENGLISH CHANNEL.

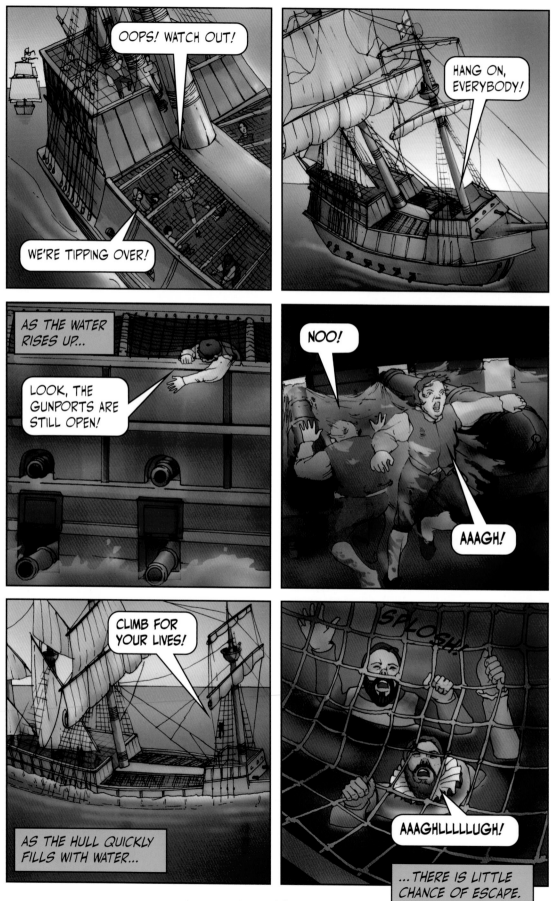

10

MAY, 1971.

HMM...AN OBJECT. WHAT IS IT?

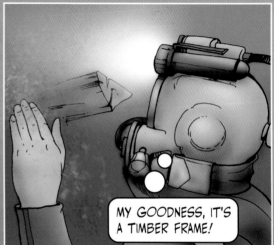

MY GOODNESS, IT'S A TIMBER FRAME!

AND ANOTHER...AND ANOTHER. THIS *COULD* BE THE MARY ROSE!

BY MARCH, 1979...

IT IS THE MARY ROSE—AN ALMOST PERFECTLY PRESERVED HALF A SHIP, FULL OF OBJECTS. AN AMAZING TIME CAPSULE OF DAYS GONE BY.

DR. MARGARET RULE, ARCHAEOLOGIST

A DECISION IS MADE TO ATTEMPT TO RAISE THE HULK.

BY 1982 ALL THE EQUIPMENT IS IN PLACE.

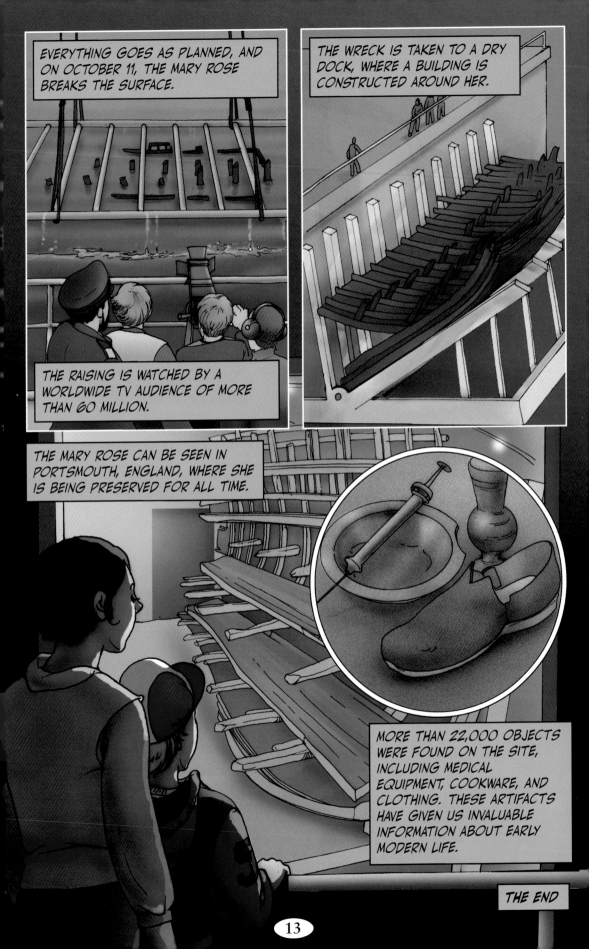

EVERYTHING GOES AS PLANNED, AND ON OCTOBER 11, THE MARY ROSE BREAKS THE SURFACE.

THE RAISING IS WATCHED BY A WORLDWIDE TV AUDIENCE OF MORE THAN 60 MILLION.

THE WRECK IS TAKEN TO A DRY DOCK, WHERE A BUILDING IS CONSTRUCTED AROUND HER.

THE MARY ROSE CAN BE SEEN IN PORTSMOUTH, ENGLAND, WHERE SHE IS BEING PRESERVED FOR ALL TIME.

MORE THAN 22,000 OBJECTS WERE FOUND ON THE SITE, INCLUDING MEDICAL EQUIPMENT, COOKWARE, AND CLOTHING. THESE ARTIFACTS HAVE GIVEN US INVALUABLE INFORMATION ABOUT EARLY MODERN LIFE.

THE END

TITANIC

IN 1985, SCIENTIST DR. ROBERT BALLARD LOCATED THE WRECK OF THE RMS TITANIC, THE GREAT LINER THAT SANK IN THE ATLANTIC OCEAN IN 1912.

ONE YEAR LATER HE RETURNS TO EXPLORE THE WRECK FURTHER...

SHE WAS STATE OF THE ART FOR HER TIME—DESIGNED TO BE PRACTICALLY "UNSINKABLE"...

THEIR SUBMERSIBLE, ALVIN, HAS BEEN SPECIALLY ADAPTED TO WORK AT A DEPTH OF OVER TWO MILES (3.2 KM) DOWN.

I'VE ALWAYS WONDERED—WHY DID SHE SINK SO QUICKLY?

WITH BALLARD ARE PILOT RALPH HOLLIS AND COPILOT DUDLEY FOSTER.

WHAT WITH HAVING 16 WATER-TIGHT COMPARTMENTS INSIDE.

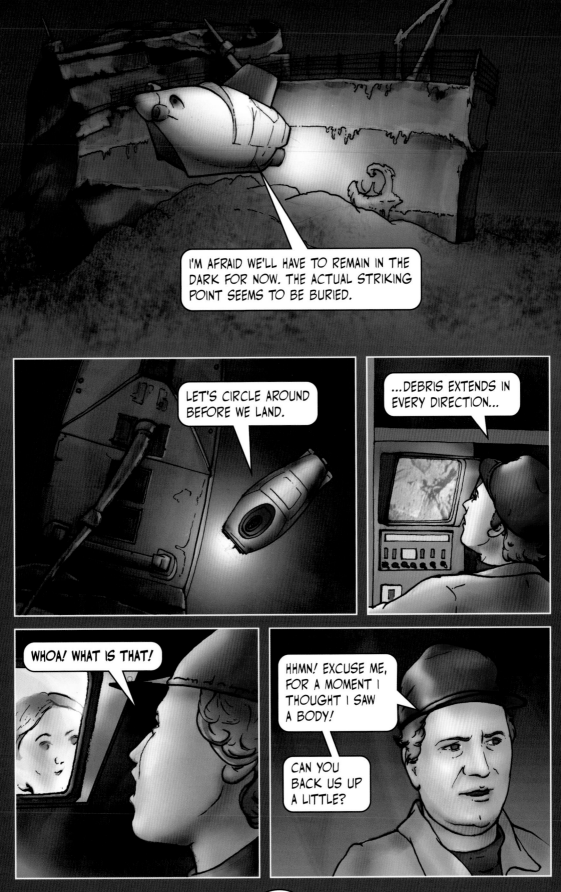

OK, TIME TO RELEASE JJ*.

*JASON JUNIOR—A ROBOTIC PROBE.

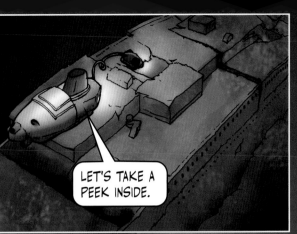

LET'S TAKE A PEEK INSIDE.

THERE IT IS—THE GRAND STAIRCASE OF WHAT WAS ONCE THE LARGEST MOVABLE OBJECT IN THE WORLD...

WIRELESS ROOM...

DOT...DOT...DASH...

...MUCH HEAVY PACK ICE ABOUT...A GREAT NUMBER OF **LARGE** ICEBERGS ARE...

...I'VE GOT SO MANY MESSAGES TO SEND—THIS WILL HAVE TO WAIT.

ON THE BRIDGE...

I *HAVE* TOLD THE CROW'S NEST TO KEEP THEIR EYES PEELED FOR GROWLERS,* SIR.

*SMALL ICEBERGS.

JAMES MOODY IS TITANIC'S SIXTH OFFICER.

EXCELLENT. THEN WE SHALL MAINTAIN PRESENT COURSE AND SPEED.

WILLIAM MURDOCH IS TITANIC'S FIRST OFFICER.

AS LONG AS IT STAYS THIS CALM, THE LOOKOUTS WILL SPOT ANY HAZARDS IN PLENTY OF TIME.

...I ACTUALLY PREFER IT A BIT ROUGHER.

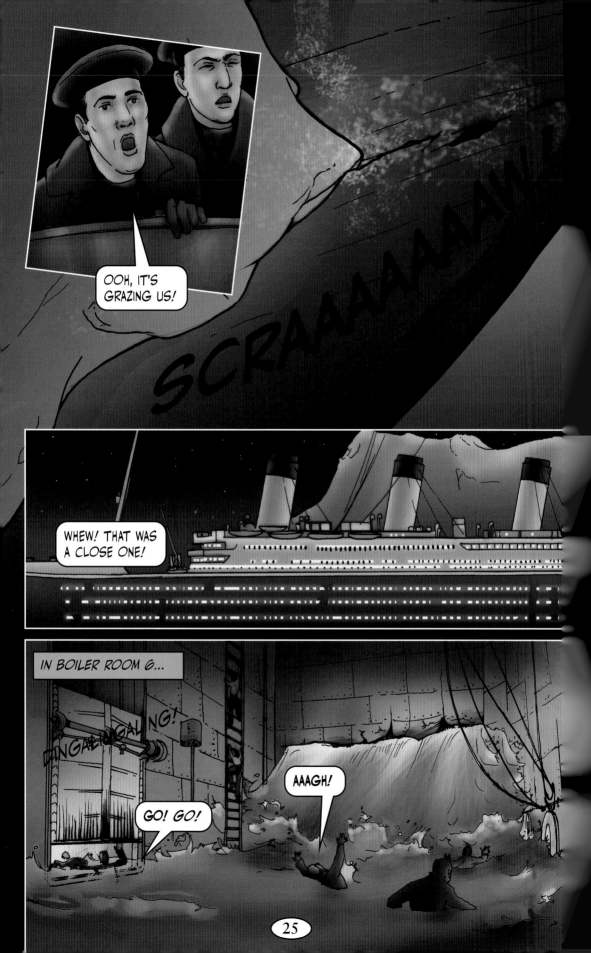

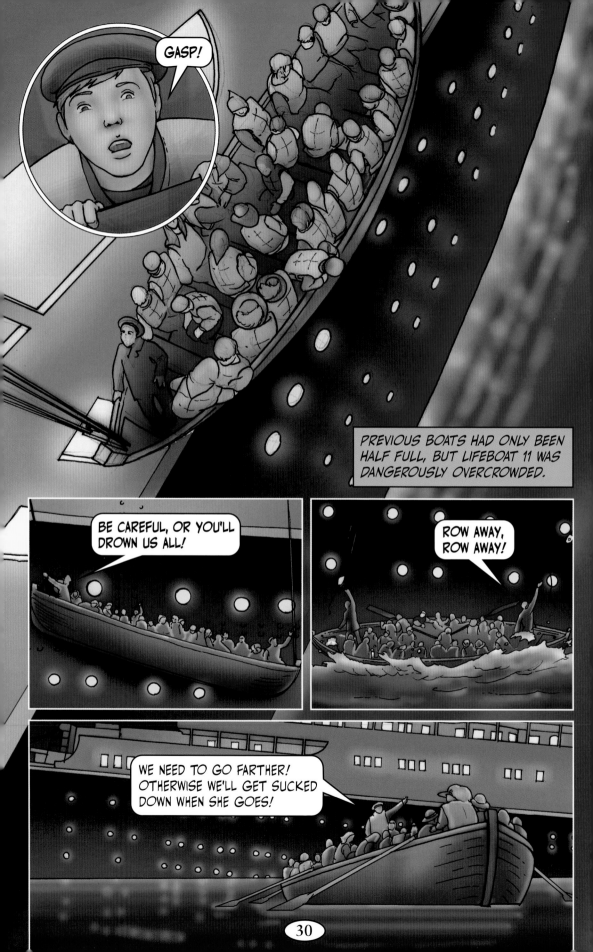

GREEEHAAW!

GALOPH!

OUT OF 2,208 PEOPLE, ONLY 712 SURVIVED.

THE LOSS OF TITANIC WAS A HUGE BLOW TO AN AGE THAT BELIEVED IN THE POWER OF TECHNOLOGY OVER NATURE.

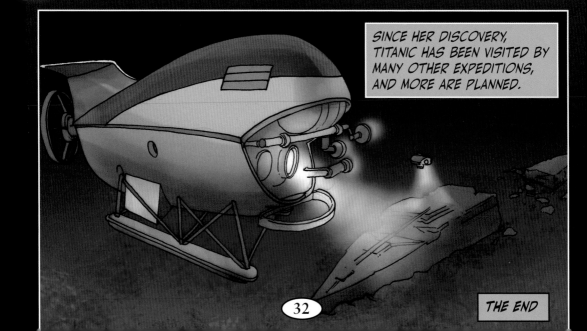

SINCE HER DISCOVERY, TITANIC HAS BEEN VISITED BY MANY OTHER EXPEDITIONS, AND MORE ARE PLANNED.

THE END

THE SINKING OF THE BISMARCK

THE GERMAN BATTLESHIP BISMARCK, THE MOST POWERFUL WARSHIP EVER MADE, HAS LEFT HER BASE IN KIEL.

MOVIETONE
INTERNATIONAL
WAR NEWS

IT IS THOUGHT THAT HER CAPTAIN, ERNST LINDEMANN, COULD BE LEADING AN ATLANTIC RAIDING PARTY UNDER THE COMMAND OF ADMIRAL GUNTHER LUTJENS.

THEIR MISSION WILL BE TO ATTACK THE CARGO SHIPS FERRYING SUPPLIES BETWEEN AMERICA AND BRITAIN.

THE BRITISH NAVY, UNDER ORDERS TO "SINK THE BISMARCK!", WILL BE DOING ALL THEY CAN TO FIND THEM FIRST...

KORSFIJORD, NORWAY, MAY 21, 1941...

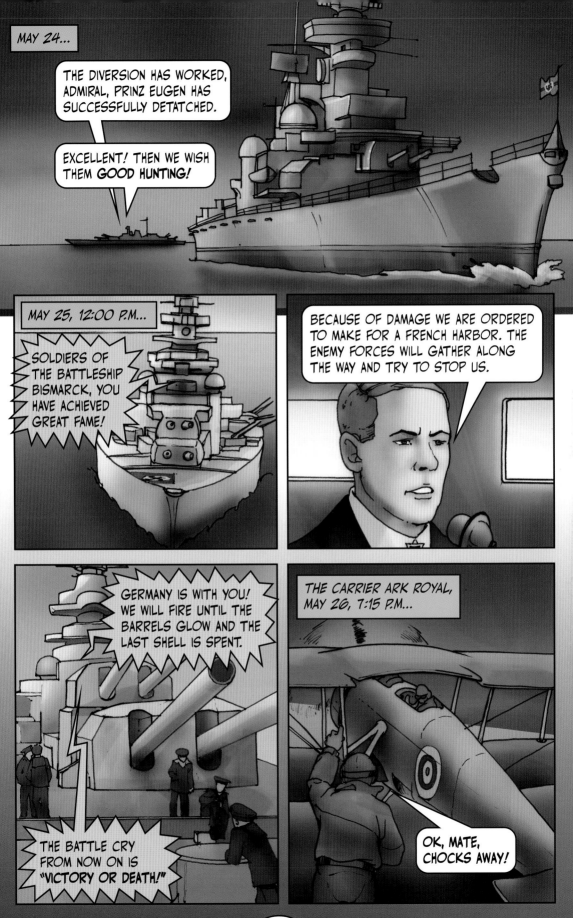

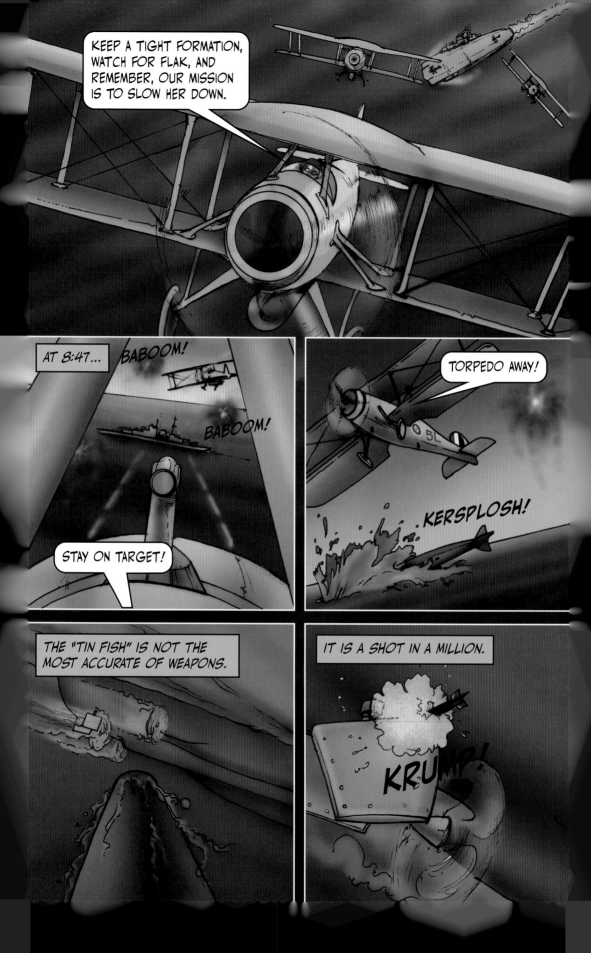

IN 2002, MOVIEMAKER JAMES CAMERON FILMED THE BISMARCK, AND MADE AN INVESTIGATION...

LET'S SEE IF IT'S TRUE THAT SHE WAS SCUTTLED BY HER OWN SAILORS.

HEY, THERE'S A BULGE! —PROBABLY FROM A TORPEDO IMPACT.

YES, BUT LOOK, THE ARMORED BELT BEHIND IS UNDAMAGED.

AMAZING! I THINK SHE COULD HAVE FLOATED FOR AT LEAST ANOTHER DAY!

ONE THING'S FOR SURE — THEY DON'T BUILD SHIPS LIKE THIS ANYMORE!

THE END

UNDERSEA ARCHAEOLOGY

A ncient shipwrecks can be a valuable source of historical information. Finding and preserving the finds requires expert knowledge and modern technology.

The side-scan sonar tow vehicle (above) sends data back to the ship's computer (below).

FINDING WRECKS

Usually historical evidence such as eyewitness accounts gives a rough idea of where a wreck might be. When they are near the site, wreck hunters use remote sensing to detect objects without having to enter the water themselves. Magnetometers can sense iron objects like nails and anchors even if they are buried beneath sediment. Unlike normal sonar, which scans the seabed from the top, side-scan sonar sends very realistic images. Sub-bottom profilers enable the viewer to see below the sediment and detect non-metallic objects that are fully buried.

The side-scan sonar can give a very clear picture of a wreck (below).

RECORDING AND PRESERVING

Once a wreck has been discovered, it has to be carefully recorded by divers or by remote-controlled submersibles. A grid of wire or metal tubes is constructed over the wreck, and drawings and photos record the finds before they are collected. The removal of items, which may appear well preserved, from the seabed, can set off a reaction that destroys them when they are exposed to the air. When items are removed from the site, they must go straight to laboratories where they can be preserved.

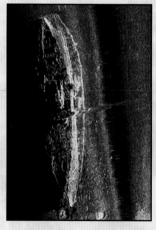

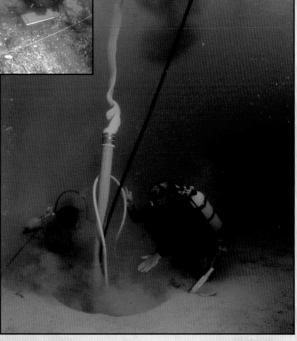

Divers make detailed recordings of a wreck before any items are removed (above right).

Sometimes sediment has to be removed from a buried wreck using a tube attached to a suction pump (right).

Items rescued from the sunken American civil war-era ironclad USS Monitor have to be carefully treated to preserve them (below).

GLOSSARY

Antarctica A continent around the South Pole entirely covered in ice.

archaeology The study of human history and prehistory through the digging up of sites that contain remains.

artifacts Man-made objects of historical interest.

capsize To overturn in water, usually resulting in a ship sinking.

compartment A separate section inside a ship.

debris Scattered pieces of a wreck.

diving bell An open-bottomed barrel or bell-shaped vessel that was waterproof. A diver could breathe the air inside while underwater. Later versions had air pumped down to them through a tube from a boat on the surface.

engraving An early form of print on paper, made from a plate of metal or block of wood that has had the image cut out or "engraved."

expedition A journey with a purpose, usually exploration or scientific.

fanciful Ideas or thoughts made up, that are not based on the truth.

gunports The openings in the side of a ship through which the guns fired. Gunports had watertight hatches.

hard–a–starboard To turn a boat quickly to the left (away from starboard–which is the right).

ice pack A large area of floating pieces of ice that are driven together to make one large floating piece. Also called pack ice.

inexperience A lack of knowledge or skill.

ironclad A 19th-century warship made of iron, or made of wood covered with plates of iron.

navigational errors Mistakes made in steering a ship in the correct direction.

obvious Clear or easy to understand.

preserving To keep the condition of something as it is.

remote-controlled To control something, like a submersible, from a distance using electronic signals such as radio waves.

sediment A layer of fine material, which can be several feet thick, that has sunk to the seabed.

sonar A device used to "see" things underwater by sending a sound signal and measuring its return. From SOund, NAvigation, and Ranging.

submersible A small craft designed to explore underwater.

FOR MORE INFORMATION

ORGANIZATIONS

Great Lakes Shipwreck Historical Society
111 Ashmun Street
Saulte Ste. Marie
Michigan 49783
(800) 635-1744
Web site: http://shipwreckmuseum.com

Discover Sea Shipwreck Museum
708 Ocean Highway
Fenwick Island
Delaware 19944
(302) 539-5524
Web site: http://www.discoversea.com

FURTHER READING

Ballard, Robert. *Finding the Titanic.* New York: Scholastic Inc, 1993.

Platt, Richard. *Eyewitness: Shipwreck.* New York: DK Children, 2000.

Porterfield, Jason. *Shipwreck: True Stories of Survival.* New York: Rosen, 2007.

Spence, David, and Susan Spence. *A History of Shipwrecks.* Milwaukee: Gareth Stevens, 2006.

INDEX

Web Sites

Due to the changing nature of Internet links, the Rosen Publishing Group, Inc., has developed an online list of Web sites related to the subject of this book. This site is updated regularly. Please use this link to access the list:

http://www.rosenlinks.com/gd/ship/